Aşk, Love, Amour

A reference of love from Turkish to English and French

Melissa Adams

Contents

Dedication i

Acknowledgment ii

About the Author...iii

Preface iv

Foreword v

Words of Love in Turkish translated to English and French ...3

Idioms 46

Proverbs 55

Dedication: Living Allegory.. 58

Research 65

Additional Research & Acknowledgement 65

Dedication

I dedicate this book to anyone who is willing to discover ourselves in a more profound way, to have the courage to unite in our differences and to find common ground in our many meanings of love.

Acknowledgment

I would like to thank a dear friend from fine arts school who proposed this idea of a project of the rumor of so many expressions of love in Turkish.

About the Author

Melissa Adams is bilingual in English and French, has a BFA with a concentration in art & science as well as a DUEF. She is a writer, an artist and has worked in entertainment.

Preface

The content of this book was researched in a city known as the gateway between the east and west. Istanbul is a fusion of linguistic and cultural influences which date back to the cradle of civilization. Turkish is an agglutinative language considered to be the most logical of languages by a computer scientist.

This book of Turkish expressions of love with translations is an attempt to begin discover our epistemology of love.

Being raised bilingual with French and English I found it fascinating to discover other languages. Turkish stems from Farsi and Arabic which are two of a few of the most ancient languages still spoken today.

I hope you enjoy it as much as I have and continue to expand our understanding of love cross culturally.

Melissa Adams

Foreword

Sometimes it is not easy to find space without judgement and be in our mind. Here, in this book about Love, we see a process that opens up room for the readers to make this emotion "love" their own. This book will take on a life of its own including not only people but also places, plants, animals and ideas; Melissa Adams kindly gives us her experiences as an artist and poet.

For some readers, this book will be amusing, for some it will be inspirational, for some a companion. The design of the book is light and delightful. It is a sparkle for our times. It is a tender call for our hearts. It delicately shows love in relation to dreams and desires. The method of writing is ethnographic and auto-ethnographic sometimes; also it resembles a contemporary dictionary suggesting a non-linear reading. She brings her wit and cleverness to our lives with her research based book.

Çiğdem Kaya, Department Chair & Professor of Industrial Design, Istanbul Technical University

"Gel, gel, ne olursan ol, yine gel,

İster kafir, ister mecusi,

İster puta tapan ol, yine gel,

Bizim dergahımız, ümitsizlik dergahı değildir,

Yüz kere tövbeni bozmuş olsan da, yine gel...

Şu toprağa sevgiden başka bir tohum ekmeyiz biz...

Beri gel, beri ! Daha da beri ! Niceye şu yol vuruculuk?

Mademki sen bensin, ben de senim, niceye şu senlik
benlik...

Ölümümüzden sonra mezarımızı yerde aramayınız!

Bizim mezarımız âriflerin gönüllerindedir."

Central Asian sufi Ebu Said-i Ebu'l-Hayr / Mevlana

Come, come, whoever you are, still come,

Whether you are an infidel or a Zoroastrian,

Whether you are an idolater, still come,

Our lodge is not the lodge of despair,

Even if you have broken your repentance a hundred
times, still come...

We do not plant any seed other than love in this soil...

Come here, come here! Even further here! What's with
the road rage?

Since you are me and I am you, why this you and me...

Do not look for our graves on the ground after our
death!

Our graves are in the hearts of the wise.

Venez, venez, qui que vous soyez, revenez,

Qu'il soit païen ou Zoroastrien,

Que vous soyez un adorateur d'idoles, revenez,

Notre loge n'est pas une loge de désespoir,

Même si tu as rompu ton repentir cent fois, reviens...

Nous ne semons que de l'amour dans ce sol...

Revenez, revenez ! Plus loin ! C'est quoi cette rage au volant?

Puisque tu es moi et que je suis toi, pourquoi ce toi et moi...

Ne cherchez pas notre tombe sur le sol après notre mort!

Notre tombe est dans le cœur des sages.

Words of Love in Turkish
translated to English and French

aşık

lover; in love, enraptured; enraptured saint, dervish,

wandering minstrel, bard, troubadour

amoureux; en amour; ravissement, saint ensorcelé,

derviche, ménestrel errant, barde, troubadour

aşıklar kahvesi

coffee lovers, coffee house of lovers, coffee house

frequented by wandering minstrels

amateurs de café, café des amoureux, café fréquenté

par des ménestrels errants

aşıkol

amorous, to fall in love with

amoureux, tomber amoureux de

aşıkl şeyda

in love with something, poet, madly in love, desperate
lover

en amour de quelque chose, poète, follement
amoureux, amoureux désespéré

aşıkyolunu şaşirmiş

embroidery meander, surprised at his love, love has lost
its way

méandre de broderie, surpris par son amour, l'amour a
perdu son chemin

aşıkl zâr

poet, tearful lover

poète, amoureux en larmes

aşkî

pertaining to love, amorous

relatif à l'amour, amoureux

aşk çocğukğu

love child

amour enfant

aşk mektubu
love letter
lettre d'amour

aşk iksiri
love potion
potion d'amour

aşk
love, passion; ecstatic love of God means ivy in arabic,
that which surrounds but does not choke
amour, la passion; amour extatique de Dieu signifie
lierre en arabe, ce qui entoure mais n'étouffe pas

aşk dolu
full of love, mainly romantic
plein d'amour, principalement romantique

aşka gelmek
great love, fall in love, come in love, you have a feeling
of loving to do something
grand amour, tomber amoureux, vient l'amour, tu as le
sentiment d'aimer faire quelque chose

aşk yapmak
to make love
faire l'amour

aşk düşmek
fall in love
tomber amoureux

aşkbaz/aişkbaz
feigning lover, gallant, coquette, flirt
amant feignant, galant, coquette, flirter

aşkim
my love, as addressed to someone
mon amour, comme adressé à quelqu'un

aşkimsin
you are my love
tu es mon amour

aşkina
for the love of, as in Allah
pour l'amour de, comme dans Allah

6

aşkiniza
to your health
santé

aşkl cismani
sensual love, carnal love
amour sensuel, amour charnel

aşkl eflâtunî
platonic love, love ethereal
amour platonique, amour éthéré

aşik et, aşik eyle
make in love
faire en amour

aşka gel, aşka gelmek
come to love, to become exulted, enraptured
venez à l'amour, venez à la réjouissance, au ravissement

aşka tutulmuş
in love with love
amoureux de l'amour

7

aşkl ilâhî
divine love
amour divin

aşk ilan etmek
declare love, profess love
déclarer l'amour, divulguer l'amour

aşk ile
with love, great zeal
avec amour, beaucoup de zèle

aşkl niyaz et
pray for love, make a supplication of love
prier pour l'amour, faire une supplication à l'amour

aşk ola
be of love, to be loved, well done, bravo
être d'amour, être aimé, bien joué, bravo

aşk olsun
let it be love
que ce soit de l'amour

aşik olmak

to fall in love

tomber amoureux

aşkl ruhanî

love spirit, spiritual love, transcendental

esprit d'amour, l'amour spirituel, transcendental

aşkla şevkle

whole-heartedly with love and enthusiasm

de tout cœur avec amour et ferveur

aşk hastasi

lovesick

amour malade

aşkbaz

feigning lover, gallant, coquette, flirt

amour feignant, galant, coquette, flirter

aşkbazlik

loveblindness, courtship

aveuglement de l'amour, courtesan

aşkin

love, philosophic transcendent

l'amour, transcendant philosophique

aşırı heyecanlı, aşırı duygusal aşk

overly excited, overly emotional love

amour exalté, excessivement émotionnel

aşkî

pertaining to love, amorous, transcendence in philosophy

relatif à l'amour, amoureuse, transcendance en philosophie

kör aşık

blind lover

amant aveugle

aşk hastasi

love sick

l'amour malade

aşk macerasi

love adventure

amour aventureux

aşti

peace, reconciliation, concord

paix, réconciliation, harmonie

aşti bahşay

peace-giving

donneur de paix

aşti hure

reconciliation feast

la paix

aşüfte

hussy, minx, jezabel, poet, besides one's self, agitated,
excited, bewildered; violently in love

coquine, friponne, jezabel, poète, en plus de soi, agité,
excité, déconcerté; violemment amoureux

aşüftelik

promiscuity, agitation, excitement, bewilderment;
passionate love

promiscuité, agitation, excitation, égarement; amour
passionné

aşk dolusu içmek

full of love, drink much love

plein d'amour, boire beaucoup d'amour

barışçıl, barışçı, barış yapma, barış yapma

pacificatory, pacifying, peacemaker

pacificatoire, pacifiant, pacificateur

bayiliyorum

i love it, adore

je l'adore, adorer

cami

mosque (arabic - place where people get together)

mosquée (arabe - l'endroit où les gens se réunissent)

cuma

friday (from cami - the day that people get together)

vendredi (de cami - le jour où les gens se rassemblent)

can

male emotional love

amour émotionnel masculine

12

canan

female emotional love

amour émotionnel féminin

canim/cânım

love (sweetie)/precious, lovely

amour (ma chérie)/précieux, charmant

canim sevgilim canim benim

my love, my soul

mon amour, mon âme

candan

sincerely, wholeheartedly; sincere, cordially, intimate

sincèrement, de tout cœur; sincère, cordialement,
intime

cani can

God, the truth of Islam, dear friend

Dieu, la vérité de l'Islam, cher ami

camu yürekten

with all one's heart and soul, most sincerely

de tout notre cœur et de toute notre âme, très

sincèrement

canimin içi

the core of my life, in my soul

le cœur de la vie, dans mon âme

cani gelip git

for one's heart to hover between hope and despair

pour que le cœur oscille entre espoir et désespoir

canim hakki için

by my soul, for the right of my life, for my darling's right

par mon âme, pour le droit de ma vie, pour le droit de

ma chérie

caninin içine sokacaği gel

to feel a strong wave of love

ressentir une forte vague d'amour

caniste

to desire

désirer

can beraber

very dear, life together

très cher, la vie ensemble

can kat

to enliven, add life, to delight greatly

pour animer, donner la vie, se faire plaisir

canâ

soul, poet, 'oh friend! darling!'

âme, poète, 'ô ami! chéri!'

canan

poet, beloved (mystical), the beloved (God)

poète, bien-aimé (mystique), le bien-aimé (Dieu)

canane

poet, beloved

poète, bien aimé

dost

friend, friendly, lover, mistress, mystical God

ami, amical, amant, maîtresse, Dieu mystique

dostdar

lover; friend

amoureux; ami

dostluk

friendship, to be friends

amitié, être amis

duygu iletişimi

emotional communication, sensually coaxing, romantic

but referring to spiritual

communication émotionnelle, sensuellement cajolant,

romantique mais se référant à la spiritualité

gönül

heart, spiritual form of heart, feelings, inclination, desire

cœur, forme spirituelle de cœur, sentiments,

inclination, désir

gönül almak

taking a heart, win the favor, to placate, to please

prendre un cœur, prends courage, apaiser, plaire

gönül bağlamak

to tie one's heart, to be attached to the heart,

to set one's heart on

lier son cœur, être attaché au cœur, y mettre son cœur

gönül eğlencesi

heart's entertainment, joy of the heart, toy of love

pour divertir le cœur, la joie du cœur, badiner avec

l'amour

gönül eğlendirmek

to have a good time, to amuse oneself, to dally

pour divertir le cœur, s'amuser

gönül kirmak

breaking hearts, to hurt someone's feelings

briser les cœurs, de blesser les sentiments de quelqu'un

gönül vermek

to give heart, to lose one's heart to, to fall for

donner du cœur, perdre son cœur pour, tomber
amoureux de

gönlü olmak

be in ones heart, to be willing, to be in love with

être dans son cœur, être disposé, être amoureux de

gönlünü almak

win your heart, to placate, to make up to

apaiser, rattraper

gönlünü etmek

to make his heart happy, to coax, to prevail on

pour rendre votre cœur heureux, amadouer, s'imposer

gönlünce

to your heart's content, after one's heart

dans votre cœur, après son cœur

gönülsüz
reluctant, half-hearted
réticent, à demi-cœur

gönül gönlümün sultani, gönül ferman dinlemiyor
sultan of my heart, does not obey orders
sultan de mon cœur, le cœur n'écoute pas les ordres

gönül iklimimin
my heart climate, the place where we live
le climat de mon cœur

gözdesi olmak
to be the favorite, to be the person that somebody likes
most in life
être le favori

güzel
good, beautiful
bon/bonne, beau/belle

güzellik
loveliness
beauté

hayatim
you are my life
chéri, ma vie, mon amour

hayatim boyunca
for all my life
pour toute ma vie

hoş
lovable, cute, nice
aimable, mignon, agréable

hoşlanmak
to find someone nice, like
trouver quelqu'un de bien, aimer

hubb, hubbub
love, affection; love of high position
amour d'affection; je peux aimer les positions élevées

hub
good, excellent, beautiful, elegant, graceful
bon, excellent, beau, élégant, gracieux, sanctuaire

habib
friend, lover, beloved
ami, amant, bien-aimé

habibe
beloved woman
femme bien-aimée

habibullah
the beloved of God, Muhammad
le bien-aimé de Dieu, Muhammad

iki gözüm
my two eyes
mes deux yeux

iki gözümün çiçeği
the flower of my two eyes
la fleur de mes deux yeux

hat/tezhip
calligraphy/illumination, spiritual
calligraphie/enluminure, spiritual

hepsini sev
love all
aimer tout

kalp
heart
cœur

kalbimdesin
you are in my heart
tu es dans mon cœur

kur
courtship, flirtation
cour, flirt

kur yapmak
courtship, to flirt
cour, flirter

maşuk
beloved, mystical God as the sole object of love, heart-
throb, sweet
bien-aimé, mystique Dieu comme seul objet d'amour,
cœur battant, doux

maşuka
beloved woman
femme bien-aimée

mahabbet, muhabbet
love, affection, friendship, friendly chat
amour, affection, amitié, conversation amicale

maşuk
beloved, mystical; God as the sole object of love
bien-aimé, mystique; Dieu comme seul objet d'amour

maşukiyet
beloved, state of being loved
mélancolie, état d'être aimé

aşk meşkl
love and romance, love affair
l'amour et la romance, affaire d'amour, affaire de cœur

muhabbetâmiz

friendly, we're in love

amicaux, nous sommes chaleureux

muhabbetârâ

love, adoring

l'amour, chérir, adorer

muhabbetkâr

loving, affectionate, conversationalist

aimant, affectueux, conversationniste

muhabbetleş

to have a loving friendship for each other; to enjoy a
friendly chat together

avoir une amitié aimante l'un pour l'autre ; pour
discuter ensemble en toute convivialité

muhabbetli

affectionate, loving; friendly correspondence

affectueux, aimant; correspondance amicale

muhabbetname, aşk mektubu, dost mektubu
love letter, letter of friendship
lettre de conversation, lettre d'amour, lettre d'ami

muhabbetzede
smitten with love, love-stricken, conversationalist
épris d'amour, frappé d'amour, conversationniste

muhaccel
placed in the wedding chamber
placé dans la chambre de mariage

muhacirîn
meccans who followed the prophet muhammad in
settling in medina; emigrants; refugees
mecquois qui ont suivi le prophète mahomet en
s'installant à médine; émigrants; réfugiés

muhibb
who loves, affectionate friend; mystical sympathizer (of
dervish & derviş orders) lover of Mevlana (love of God)
qui aime, affectionnera l'ami; mystère sympathisant (du
derviche & derviş ordres) amoureux de Mevlana
(amour de Dieu)

mahbube
the beloved woman
femme bien-aimée

mahbub
beloved of the whole world
bien-aimé du monde entier

mahiyet
the reality; true nature of a thing; character; entity;
essence
la réalité; la vraie nature d'une chose; personnage;
entité; essence

mahfuk
affected with palpitations of the heart; bereft of reason;
mad
affecté de palpitations cardiaques; privé de raison; fou

mahaşerallah / inşallah
whom God has assembled together; very crowded, God willing
que Dieu a rassemblé; très fréquenté, si Dieu le veut

maşallah
wonderful, magnificent, praise be;
current for protection of devil eyes
merveilleux, magnifique, loué soit; courant pour la
protection des yeux du diable

muhabbetkuşu
lovebirds
inséparables

muhibban
friends, loved ones
amis, proches

muhibbane
friendly, affectionately
amical, affectueux

nefes
breath, which has healing power that is blown on the
sick - poem sung by dervishes
souffle, qui a un pouvoir de guérison qui est soufflé sur
les malades - poème chanté par les derviches

sifir-sifir
love all , losing oneself in another - Sufi
aimer tout, se perdre dans l'autre - Soufi

sana tapiyourm
i adore you
je t'adore

sevgi ile
lovingly
avec amour

benimile sevismek
make love with me
fais l'amour avec moi

sev
to love; to like; to pet, fondle, caress
adorer, aimer, câliner, cajoler, caresser

sev yeter
just love, love is enough
j'aime juste, l'amour suffit

sevadül kalb

love heart, the black core supposed to exist in the heart

cœur d'amour, le noyau noir censé exister dans le cœur

sevadül müslimin

the general mass of Muslims

la majorité des Musulmans

sevecen

loving, caressing, compassionate, kind

aimant, caresser, compatissant, gentil

sevap

good love, good deed

bon amour, bonne action

sevap kazanmak

to earn merit, earning good deeds

gagner du mérite,

sevaptır

it is a good deed

c'est une bonne action

sevaba girmek

enter into good deeds, to acquire merit in Gods sight

entrer dans de bonnes actions, pour acquérir du mérite

aux yeux de Dieu

sevgiyle kalin, hoşçakalın

stay with love, good bye

reste avec amour, au revoir

asklarin en guzeli

the most beautiful of loves

le plus beau des amours

sevda

love, to be passionately in love; intense longing; strong

wish or desire; melancholy, spleen, black bile

intense longing for power, ambition; greed for gain;

scheme, project; trade, commerce, business

amour, être passionnément amoureux, désir intense,

souhait ou désir fort;

mélancolie, spleen, bile noire

désir intense de pouvoir, ambition, avidité de gain, plan,

projet, commerce, affaires, commerce, affaires

sevda çekmek

to be deeply in love, passionately, suffer the pangs of
passionate love

être profondément amoureux, passionnément, souffrir
les affres de l'amour passionné

sevdasina düşmek

to become imbued with a passion for, develop a
passionate desire to fall in love

s'imprégner d'une passion pour, développer un désir
passionné de tomber passionnément amoureux de

sevdalanmak

to fall passionately in love with

tomber amoureux

sevdaperest

love-loving, slave to his own desires; ambitious, sensual

affectueux, esclave de ses propres désirs ; ambitieux,
sensuel

sevdavî

love, amiable, melancholic, atrabilious; amorous;
pertaining to the black bile

amour, aimable, mélancolique, atrabilaire; amoureux;
relevant de la bile noire

kara sevdali

in love, black - no light, somber lover

amoureuse/amoureux, noir – pas de lumière, amant sombre

sevdali

lover, enamored, love sick, in love, tender, love struck,
madly in love; person who is passionately in love,
person who's passionately fond of something
colloquial; man who loves a prostitute and who is
genuinely loved by her in return

amant, épris, malade d'amour, amoureux, tendre,
amoureux frappé, follement amoureux; personne qui
est passionnément amoureuse, personne qui est
passionnément friande de quelque chose familier;
homme qui aime une prostituée et qui est sincèrement
aimé par elle en retour

sevdalanmak

to fall in love; to lose one's heart

tomber amoureux; perdre son cœur

sevdazede

fondness, in deep love; melancholic

affection, dans un amour profond; mélancolique

sevdirmek

to make love or let be loved, liked or fondled, endearing

faire l'amour ou laisser être aimé, aimé ou caressé, attachant

sevgi

love, affection, compassion

amour, affection, compassion

sevgili

beloved

bien-aimé

sevgilim

my love

mon amour

sevgilerimie

at the end of a letter, love; affectionately yours

à la fin d'une lettre, amour; affectueusement vôtre

sevgilerle

with love

avec amour

sevi

archaic love, affection, compassion, current love

equal; uniform; even, level; straight, erect (2 minarets);

passionate love, love

amour archaïque, affection, compassion, amour actuel

égal; uniforme; égal, niveau; droit, érigé (2 minarets);

amour passionné, amour

sevici

lover, love emotional and spiritual for every person

amant, l'amour émotionnel et spirituel pour chaque

personne

sevicilik

endearment, sapphism, emotional, spiritual love for

every person

attachement, saphisme, amour émotionnel et spirituel

pour chaque personne

sevgili

beloved; dear, darling, loveable

bien-aimé; cher, chéri, adorable

sevgili arkadaşım

my dear friend

mon cher ami

sevgili kadın

beloved woman

femme bien-aimée

sevim

love, affection; affability, charm

amour d'affection; affabilité, charme

sevimli

loveable, affable; general, charming, lovely, cute

aimable, affable; général, charmant, charmant, mignon

sevinç

joy, pleasure, delight

joie, plaisir, délice

sevincinden yere basamamak

unable to step down from your joy, to be overwhelmed
with joy

incapable de descendre de ta joie, être submergé de joie

sevinçli

joyful

joyeux

sevinçle

joyfully

joyeusement

sevindim

i am pleased, i am happy

je suis satisfait, j'en suis ravie

sevindir, sevindirmek, memnun etmek, mutlu etmek
to please, make happy
pour plaire, rendre heureux

sevinmek
to feel glad, feel happy, rejoice
se sentir heureux, se sentir heureux, réjouir

sevmek
to love, to like, to fondle, caress
aimer, aimer, caresser, caresser

sevmek istiyorum
i want to love
je veux aimer

sevişmek
to love or caress one another, to make love; to like one
another, to be good friends
s'aimer ou se caresser, faire l'amour; s'aimer, être de
bons amis

sevilen
loved, popular
aimée, populaire

seviyorum

i love

j'aime

sevdali kara

black, no light; loved land

noir, pas de lumière; aimer le noir

sevdali

madly in love; melancholic, monomaniacal; lovesick, a man

who loves a prostitute and he is loved by her in return

follement amoureux; mélancolique, monomaniaque;

amour malade, un homme qui aime une prostituée et

qui l'aime en retour

sevgi dolu

full of love

plein d'amour

sevgi dolu olma

warmheartedness, being full of love

chaleur humaine, être plein d'amour

sevgi dolu bir halde

warmly, adoringly, in a loving state

chaleureusement, avec adoration, dans un état d'amour

sevgi dolu şekilde

tenderly, in a loving way

tendrement, de manière aimante

sevgi dolu bir şekilde

dotingly, in a loving manner

affectueusement, de façon aimante

sevgi gosteren

one who shows love, affectionate

quelqu'un qui montre de l'amour, de l'affection

sevgiyle anilan

cherished, loved, fondly remembered

avoir été chéri(e), aimé(e), un souvenir impérissable

sevgiyle anmak

cherish, remembering with love

chérir, se souvenir avec amour

sevgi duymak

love, to feel love, yearn, care for

aimer, un goût prononcé pour le désir, pour le ressenti

amoureux

seven

loving

aimant

sevecan

loving, tender, compassionate

bienveillant, tendre, compatissant

seni seviyorum

i love you

je t'aime

sevgili

lover, beloved

amant, bien-aimé

sevgilim

my love, darling

mon amour, chéri(e)

sevisme
lovemaking, physical
faire l'amour

cok sevmek
adore, to love very much
adorer, aimer beaucoup

sultani
sultan of every part of my heart, soul
sultan de chaque partie de mon cœur, âme

tapmak
to worship, to adore; i worship you to the ends of the
earth
adorer, vénérer; je t'adore jusqu'aux extrémités de la
terre

tapinmak
to worship, to adore
vénérer, adorer

taaşşuk
falling in love; to fall in love with
tomber amoureux; tomber amoureux de

ta'atuf
being kind and affectionate to each other, sympathy
être gentils et affectueux l'un envers l'autre, sympathie

tab
illuminating, shining, glowing, as in from fire
twisting, spinning, as in one who weaves
illuminant, brillant, luisant, comme un feu ondulant,
filant, comme quelqu'un qui tisse

tenasül
reproduction
rapports sexuels

tutku
passion, crush
la passion, béguin

tutkulu
passionate
passionné

tutkun
in love, smitten with, nuts over
passionnés, amoureuse, éprise de, folle de

tutkulu asik
passionately in love
passionnément amoureux

tutkunluk
passion, love, amorousness, admiration, captivity,
infatuation, affinity, gloat, heartthrob, addiction
(medical), amorously
passion, amour, amourette, admiration, captivité,
infatuation, affinité, jubilation, coup de cœur,
dépendance (médicale), amoureusement

tutulmak
be smitten with, be in love with
être épris de, être amoureux de

yar, sevgili
darling, beloved
chéri(e), bien-aimé

yâr
love, friend, lover, one's beloved; helper
amour, ami(e), amant, bien-aimé; l'aidant

yârü agyar
friend and foe, all the world
amis et ennemis, dans le monde entier

yâri cân
dear soul, the beloved, lover of life, lover of heaven
chère âme, le bien-aimé, amoureux de la vie, amoureux
au paradis

yârl gâr
intimate friend; companion in adversity
ami intime; compagnon dans l'adversité

yârl kadîm
an old friend
un ancien ami(e)

yârol
to be loving friends with one another; to be a helping
friend, to assist
d'être des amis affectueux les uns envers les autres;
d'être un ami aidant, d'assister

yârolup bâr olma
to be a friend without making oneself burdensome
être un ami sans se rendre pénible

yârl vefadar
loyal friend
ami fidèle

yârü yaver ol
to help and favor one another
s'entraider et se favoriser mutuellement

Idioms

aşkın gözü kördür
love is blind
l'amour est aveugle

iki sevgili, kumrular gibi sevisen iki kisi
two lovers, two people making love like lovebirds
deux amants, deux personnes faisant l'amour comme
des tourtereaux

ilk goruste asik olmak
love at first sight
le coup de foudre

sevilir, sevimli, cana yakin hoş
likeable, lovable, friendly, pleasant
sympathique, aimable, amical, agréable

aşk tanrisi, küpid; psik. eros
God of love, cupid; psych. eros
Dieu de l'amour, cupidon; psy. éros

aşkina, hatiri için
for the love of, for the sake of
pour l'amour de

aşk elması
love diamond, love apple
diamant d'amour, pomme d'amour

hippilerin taktıkları birkaç sıra boncuktan oluşan kolye
love beads, a necklace of several rows of beads worn by
hippies
perles d'amour, collier de plusieurs rangs de perles
porté par les hippies

aşk husule getiren büyü, (hiç say)
magic that creates love, (never count)
la magie de l'amour, (ne jamais compter)

dostluk bağlarini kutlayan ve kuvvetlendiren ziyafet
love feast, banquet celebrating and strengthening the
bonds of friendship
fête de l'amour, banquet célébrant et renforçant les
liens d'amitié

muhabbet alâmeti olarak hisisî bir şekilde bağlana

şyonga

love knot, a link that connects emotionally as a sign of

affection

nœud d'amour, un lien qui se connecte sensuellement

en signe d'affection

yalnız aşk üzerine kurulan izdivaç

love match, a marriage built on love alone

un mariage fondé uniquement sur l'amour

aşk hikâyesi, aşk romani

love story, romance novel

histoire d'amour, roman d'amour

aşk ve alâka gösterme

love suit, showing love and affection

montrer de l'amour et de l'affection

aşk-olmayinca meşk

love-when there is no love

l'amour quand il n'y a pas d'amour

sen benim hayatımın anlamısın

you are the meaning of my life

tu es le sens de ma vie

sevgi emeği

labor of love

travail d'amour

abayi yakmak, âşik olmak

to fall in love, to be in love

tomber amoureux, être amoureux

bir kiza âşik olmak

falling in love with a girl

tomber amoureux d'une fille

aşkimin hatiri için

for the sake of my love

dis mon amour, envoie mon amour

sevgilerimi söyle, sevgilerimi ilet

tell my love, convey my love

relate mon amour, transmets mon amour

aşk kuşları, muhabbetkuşu

love birds (doves), parakeet

oiseaux d'amour (tourtereaux), perruche

cörekotu (botanik)

love in a mist (botanical)

l'amour dans la brume (botanique)

yabanî menekşe (botanik)

hearts ease, love in idleness (botanical)

soulagement du cœur, l'amour dans l'oisiveté

(botanique)

horozibiği çiçeği (botanik)

love lies bleeding (botanical)

l'amour saigne (botanique)

tılsım, aşk kilidi

amulet, love lock

talisman, serrure d'amour

sevgilisi taraşndan birakilmiş, terkedilmiş; aşk hicrani
çeken
love lorn, abandoned and deserted by her lover;
suffering from the agony of love
malheureux en amour, abandonnée et délaissée par son
amant ; souffrant des affres de l'amour

güzel, latif, hoş, sevimli, sevilir
beautiful, pleasant, pleasant, lovely, lovable, lovable
beau, agréable, agréable, charmant, aimable, aimable

güzellik, sevimlilik
beauty, loveliness
beauté, charme

âşik, seven kimse, dost
lover, one who loves, friend
amoureux, celui qui aime, ami

sanat âşiği
art lover
amateur d'art

aşkiyle vurulmuş - birisinin

love struck, of someone smitten with love

amour ardent, d'une personne éprise d'amour

seven, sevgi gösteren, müşşk

loving, showing love, affection

aimer, montrer de l'amour, de l'affection

iki kulplu büyük içki kâsesi, mükâfat olarak verilen kâse

loving cup, drink bowl with two handles, a bowl given as
a reward

coupe d'amour, un grand bol à boire avec deux anses,
un bol donné en récompense

şefkat, lütfen, iyilik, merhamet

compassion, please, favour, mercy

compassion, s'il vous plaît, faveur, miséricorde

sevgi tavri

attitude of love

attitude d'amour

ustune gul koklamamak

not to smell another rose when with a person, not to

cheat on a lover

ne pas sentir une autre rose quand on est avec

quelqu'un, ne pas tromper son amant

birtanem

my dearest one

mon seul et unique

can yoldasi

life partner

compagnon de vie

ruh eşim

my soul mate

mon âme sœur

gönül vermek

give one's heart to

donner du cœur à

göz koymak

to pursue, to have an eye on, to desire

poursuivre, garder un œil sur, désirer

gönlünü kaptirmak

be smitten with, be infatuated with, fall in love with, lose

one's heart to, be head over heels with, being carried

away

s'éprendre de, s'enticher de, tomber amoureux de,

perdre son cœur pour, être ébloui par, être transporté

par

başinda kavak yelleri esmek

daydreaming, having one's head in the clouds,

consumed by thoughts of one's love, seeing nothing but

only one person, as if not sober

rêvasser, avoir la tête dans les nuages, être absorbé par

les pensées de son amour, ne rien voir d'autre qu'une

seule personne, comme si l'on n'était pas sobre

aşk husule getiren büyü

love spell

sortilège de l'amour

Proverbs

aşık kalemi kör, dört yanını duvar sanır

the lover's world is blind and they think that they are
surrounded by walls

le monde des amoureux est aveugle, que tout autour
d'eux des murs sont érigés

aşığa Bağdat sorulmaz Irak, uzak değildir

as the center of science and knowledge a lover is not
asked about Baghdad, Irak is not too far

en tant que centre de la science et de la connaissance,
un amoureux n'est pas interrogé sur Bagdad, l'Irak n'est
pas si loin

aşıka ya sabir ya sefer gerek

the lover needs either patience or expedition

l'amant a besoin de patience ou d'expédition

aşıkin hali kalinden belli olur

the state of the lover is evident from the heart

l'état de l'amant est visible dans son cœur

aşıkolan karda gezer, izini belli etmez

the one in love walks in the snow, not showing his trace

l'amoureux marche dans la neige, sans montrer sa trace

aşıka rüsvaylik dendi belâsidir

the beloved is called the scourge of humiliation

le bien aimé est nommé comme le fléau de
l'humiliation

aşk-ağlatir, dert söyletir

love makes you cry, trouble makes you talk, sing

l'amour fait pleurer, les ennuis font parler, chanter

aşk olmayinca meşk olmaz

there's no love without love; without love and
enthusiasm no real mastership can be attained

ill n'y a pas d'amour sans amour; sans amour et sans
enthousiasme, aucune véritable maîtrise ne peut être
atteinte

"bütün güzel kadinlar zannettiler ki aşk üstüne yazdiğim
her şiir kendileri için yazilmiştir"

    - O.V. Kanik

all the beautiful women thought every poem I write
about love written for themselves
toutes les belles femmes ont pensé que chaque poème
que j'ai écrit leur étaient destinés

can elden gitmeyince canan ele giremez
if life is not lost, the beloved cannot be found
si la vie n'est pas perdue, l'être aimé ne peut pas être
retrouvé

"yurt aşki bilim aşki gönlüm düştü bu gel gör beni aşk
neyledi"

    - Yunus Emre

love of home, love of science, my heart fell in this love;
come and see what love has done to me
l'amour de la maison, l'amour de la science, mon coeur
est tombé dans cet amour viens voir ce que l'amour a
fait de moi

Dedication: Living Allegory

A living allegory of last names collected in the order I
met people on my journey of collecting the words of
love of Turkish in Istanbul. Turkish people picked their
last names 100 years ago with a specific meaning:

Go to war, rock;

Trustworthy rock;

Cheerfulness, gladness I am his rock.

Aspiration;

Coming inside.

Name of a river: survivor;

Made from light;

Wish for happiness;

Something that lives, alive.

Old Turkish emperor.

The first letter of the Arabic alphabet;
Trustworthy Hero;

Queen.

Evolution;
Hard shell,
Tree bark;
Spiritual permission,
Iron.
Rebel warriors that fought in Aegean region,
"The one born in the sky" or "the child of the sky" or
"sky born".

Sun;

The apple of my eye,
The son of a cornel.

November;
Describer,

Commander,

King of the sky,
Blame.

Kind of flower,

Pure,
real,
life.
Someone who is important for his country;
to jump into something with swords.

Magical woman;

Angel.
Place by the hill;

The place where friends meet,

The place by the fires,

The building in which they live;

Honor,

Bold,

The iron essence.

Perfume,

Nice smell,

Scent,

Essence,

Geranium.

Being about to cry.

Young male camel.

An ancient Turkish society from middle Asia;

Moving something or someone from here to there,
world.

The name of the empire, Çağatay.

Unic, nobody resembles him.

Oil lamp.
Arabic for sound.

Green branch;

Good smell,
A sacrifice.

Princess;
People who live near the Firat river.

Sea of bitterness.

Persian queen from Samaria;
Best or very good knowledge and make him a king.

Star,
River,

Bird,

Sea.

Last rose.

Falcon spring.

Gracious gift from god;

The essence of something,

To pull something.

Flower,

Get used.

Revolution,

Lots of knowledge.

Big kings.

Sends everyone happiness;

Full moon,

strong,

budun.

In loving memory of my time in Istanbul with you and your help with this love project, I am grateful for all of your graciousness!

Special thanks to the Kaya family!

Research

- Ottoman and Turkish dictionaries; Library of Ataturk
- Ottoman and Turkish dictionaries; Library of the Ahmed III

Additional Research & Acknowledgement

- Professor Çiğdem Kaya
- Emine Kaya & Sefer Kaya
- Professor Dr. Yekta Saraç
- Seda Yeşildal
- Salt Beyoğlu, Vasıf Kortun
- KATALIST, Bahadir Güzel & Fahri Ozkaramanli

And word of mouth from friends I met along the way.

www.ingramcontent.com/pod-product-compliance
Lightning Source LLC
Chambersburg PA
CBHW051238120626
46547CB00013B/1693